*SILENCE SPEAKS*

*BY: MELISSA FELIX M.ED.*

Published by Rhoyal Scribe Publishing

ISBN: 979-8-218-86268-8

Printed in the United States of America

First Edition---November 2025

# _FOR YOU_

# *ACKNOWLEDGEMENTS*

***To my mom and dad:*** *Thank you for always encouraging me, believing in me and being my biggest cheerleaders.*

***To my Grandma Flo:*** *Thank you for being my best friend, confidant and the epitome of a Proverbs 31 woman. You are missed greatly. I pull on your strength, poise, and love for life daily...you're loved forever and always.*

***To my Grandpa Charles:*** *Thank you for teaching me the power of discipline, self-control and the love of baking. As you always said, "Bye for now".*

***To my dear Mother Dorothy Leonard:*** *My passion for education and laughter in the classroom comes from you. The constant reminder of "it's gonna be alright" is in my ear. You are missed and will forever be in my heart.*

***To Lisa Thompson:*** *From Upward Bound to adulthood...thank you for always supporting me and being a listening ear.*

***To my Bonus family, my best friends, my support system:*** *Thanks for your support during the toughest years of my life. Thanks for doing life with me.*

***To Kandace Nollie:*** *Thank you for helping me heal as I journey through this thing called life.*

# *DEDICATION*

*To all women, mothers, and anyone who has experienced loss.*

*To anyone who has dealt with low self-esteem.*

*To anyone who has had a hard time conceiving.*

*To anyone who dealt with infertility alone.*

*To anyone who has ever felt unseen, unheard, or misunderstood.*

*To anyone who had to do motherhood in an unconventional way.*

*To anyone who has overcome obstacles too hard for their minds to comprehend, yet they still made it through.*

*To anyone who has ever suffered in silence.*

*You*
*Are*
*Not*
*Alone.*

*This book is for you.*

# NOTE TO THE READER

*I chose to create this collection of poetry to express my journey, my narrative, and my essence. I began writing poetry when I found out I had Premature Ovarian Failure. This is when a woman's ovaries stop working, and no longer produce eggs, much earlier than normal. I found this out at the age of 36 although, I suspect it all began in my late 20s. Doctor after doctor, from state to state, would tell me that the "symptoms" I was experiencing were just "stress". I never knew what they called "stress" would actually leave me baby-less. Devastation and pain ran through my entire body when I found out the news. I felt like something that I never had was ripped from my body, torn away and never to be returned. I felt robbed. I felt ashamed. I felt unworthy and not good enough. I cried out the feelings of unfairness.*

*I screamed out "WHY" in anger, frustration and hurt. It was the encouragement of my support system that helped me see a glimpse of hope and a small ray of sunshine. Writing was my way of getting through sleepless nights and moments of emotional outpours. It was and continues to be therapeutic healing for me. I was blessed to be able to share my story on a few platforms. It was through this time of sharing that I realized that I wasn't out here alone. It was through stories shared to me by other women privately, that made me want to share my story publicly and no longer suffer in silence as many of us do. So, join me as I share my life, my world, my ups, my downs, my tears and triumphs...my story.*

*Silence is no longer silent.*

*Silence Speaks.*

# TABLE OF CONTENTS

## WHISPERS OF AN EMPTY NEST

## THE HEARTBEAT OF HOPE

## ECHOES OF THE MIND

## SONGS OF THE HEART UNFOLDING

## *THE VOICE RISING*

# _WHISPERS OF AN EMPTY NEST_

*After sharing my story with the community at large, a
multitude of women began to share their support and their
own personal stories with me. One connection that we all had
was the reality of the feeling of loneliness on this journey and
living through it silently.*

*Infertility can be hard to talk about especially if you don't
feel heard and understood.*

*Some people take silence as being antisocial, those of us who
live with silence may see it as protecting the little bit of peace
that we have left.*

*Sometimes it's easier not to share, not to vent,
instead—just—-be—-silent.*

*The reality is Silence really isn't silent.*

# *<u>SILENCE SPEAKS</u>*

When the emotion of Silence overcomes you, it speaks so
loudly
that your soul's tears descend from your eyes in a raging
crescendo of despair.
Your heart races in an expeditious onslaught of
serendipitous regret.
Untamed thoughts, exhausted from echoes uncontrollably
running rampant through your mind
as you try to push back tears, determined to trickle down
your expectations sublime.

Silence is an emotion.
One that I know so dearly.
It's so hard to express it, because it doesn't come out
clearly.
It wraps its arms around you
and won't let go
As much as you try to shake it
No one will ever know.
No one knows the pains at night
Or random thoughts throughout the day
No one knows how much silence torments you When
your thoughts and feelings are at play.

Silence is an emotion.

One that I know very well
That's why I do my best to take my story and tell.
You sit alone
Trying to stop the tears from falling
You sit with others
Trying to maintain a smile—
all while disappearing.
Clinging to the appearance of happiness
But truly feeling sadness.
The loss of a baby
That you've never even
conceived
The longing for that baby
That represents---me.

When silence creeps up on me
I truly don't know what to do.
I cry and stress
Deep thoughts arise
I wait for Silence to hide.
Away from my mind, my body, my soul.

I hate to just be still.
Still with my thoughts, my emotions, my…silence.
It can be so quiet yet loud when going through it all alone.
Silence be still, be quiet.
This…Silence…speaks…so…loudly
.

I truly wish it didn't.
But this sound just won't go quiet,
Its Silence Speaks deafening
How I long to embrace this
vision
A vision of me, with child,
A mom.

*As an educator, I have seen many students in my classrooms and throughout the hallways.*
*I sometimes see parents take these precious minds for granted. There are times when parents complain about the child or children that they have and meanwhile I see them as simply blessings that I wish I had.*
*Life is precious.*
*Those in your lives are precious too.*
*Be blessed.*
*Be Thankful.*

# ***DON'T TAKE IT FOR GRANTED***

Don't take it for granted
To be able to birth life.

Don't take it for granted
To be able to have a baby.

Don't take it for granted
To be able to watch your baby grow into a child.

Don't
Take
It
For
Granted.

*Premature Ovarian Failure, also known as P.O.I., is a type of infertility in which a woman no longer has any eggs. Doctor after doctor continued to tell me that the symptoms that I was exhibiting were "just stress".*

*I finally found a doctor in Virginia who listened, cared and ultimately helped me find out what was to be my new reality. I found out that I had no eggs. I was not going to be able to have my own biological baby.*

*I was infertile.*
*I am infertile.*
*I am 1 in 5 women who are infertile.*

# *PREMATURE OVARIAN FAILURE*

It's been described as a nightmare, but in my humble
opinion; it's worse.
Because you see in this situation, I can't wake up.
I can't just sit up and shake it off knowing it wasn't
the result of an unhealthy diet or eating too many
sweets… Just some figment of my sleepy imagination.

This.
What I am dealing with came straight from the experts.
My doctor.
I'm living with Premature Ovarian Failure—
And there's no fixing it.

It's a thief, the worst possible kind.
It quite literally stole my ability to have my own child.

My bad and good days are starting to blur— to the point
where I really can't tell.
I'm always on the brink of tears and I never know what
will trigger me into a breakdown.

And when it happens, I don't just go back to normal.

The sadness lingers and so I struggle through trying to keep up
appearances for the people around me.
My friends, my family, my students, my co-workers.
I try to be "normal", but I'm drastically failing.
Just—keep—smiling.
Smile through the torrential rains
that flow out my eyes from all the pain.
Smile through the dark clouds of hurt and sadness
that hover above me.
Smile as my heart wails out for my unconceivable baby.

You see, smiling isn't as easy as it seems.
It literally takes strength and ability.
I'm doing my best,
Perhaps not good enough
Because the pain that I feel inside is having a hard time not
showing up.

On my face, this smile is like a mask.
A mask that is covering the essence of my being.
Just—being—me.
Who is hiding from the reality
That what I always longed for is no longer there.
And the only way to get it there Is by
retrieving a donated egg.
Egg.
This egg.
This donated egg.

The ultimate gift.
This egg will be fertilized and set inside of me to
be nurtured and cared for is my plea.
This egg will grow inside of me and become a small being.
So, I sit and wait.
Wait for the day that this dream that I have will turn into
reality.
And I will one day birth this bundle of joy—this egg.
I may not be able to carry **my own** baby, but my doctors
say I can carry **a** baby.
You know how most people wish and pray for money or
lottery winnings?
I just want pregnancy.

# ***FERTILE***

Nature pours its tears onto this Earth
I shine my sunrays upon it

Winter comes
It's still and quiet
The ground is cold
Nothing rising from it

That which is underneath lies asleep and dormant
The seeds that seem to hibernate continue to make me wait
I keep working, as only the Earth can do
Praying to see brighter days for me and for you

I take the sun and hide it nicely
Behind the clouds offering a glimmer of hope
Take a look at the ground,
Anything blooming?
Nope.

Birds are chirping
As they fly through my breeze
I blow the clouds so slightly
Just so the world can see
The ray of sunshine
That brings my inner desires to a somber peace.

It's Spring
The ground feels my tears coming from the clouds
I'm hoping it will wake those seeds up
If not, I'm going to shout!

Anger strikes loudly
As lightning hits the ground
Why nothing is happening is a mystery
Will I ever find out?

Summer's here
I can feel the heat
"It's definitely baking underneath",
I think.

I can't shed as many tears
I already saturated Spring with most of my
worries, doubts and fears.

This ground is super dry
I feel like giving up
Why bother to try?
The birds don't like chirping in my hot wind.
Rainbows only show up when I've almost given in.
The scorched grass reminds me it could be the end.
But maybe below the parched ground that we see
Perhaps just maybe those seeds are still baking

So I weep a little more as the clouds let them fall
Wishing they'll reach that which may be no more

Fall comes
There's a change in how I make the trees sway and flow
The calm of my energy,
The way the leaves blow
Hear them as they crunch under one's feet
They glide through my soft push
As I sit in thought
Hoping, wishing at least one seed awakens up
The only things that have sprung are those tree stumps
from afar
That seed I've been waiting for
Has long been gone
It's no more
Nothing's there
Don't bother to look

As my tree branches hang low
The sun still sits high
The stars continue to sparkle at night
And although I feel disconnected
I am still
Connected
Rooted
My love is unwavering
To the One who sits above

The One who's watching and waiting

To see how I move
How I deal with what I feel is a tragedy
This gut-wrenching thing,
called,
Infertility.

# *ONE*

I always wanted to have a large family.
I wanted to have 7 kids.
At first, I wanted all boys.
When I got older, I wanted a combination of boys and girls.
Now, I just want
O
N
E.
One baby to call my own.
O
N
E.
That number seems so small, so simple, not too much to
ask for,
But the day I found out that I had Premature Ovarian
Failure was the day I asked,
"Not one? Not one egg?"
Nope, not one.
It was in that moment that I watched my dreams get swept
away in the river of my tears.
Who would've thought the number one would change my
world so drastically?

All I want is
        O
        N
        E.

*Merriam Webster describes empathy as "the action of understanding, being aware of, being sensitive to, and vicariously experiencing the feelings, thoughts, and experience of another".*

*Sometimes when people try to relate or empathize, they express how they have gone through similar situations as you. As someone who lives with infertility, many times I would prefer a listening ear, a shoulder to cry on, tissue, understanding and just to be heard.*

*It would even be appreciated if one is asked how they want to be supported in those moments. Listen to understand instead of listening to respond—it makes a difference.*

# *IT'S NOT THE SAME*

"I have what you have. I can't have kids either."
"Change your diet and eat more vegetables. That will do it."
No, we are not the same.
No, IT is NOT the same.
A doctor says, "You won't be able to have a biological baby
of your own."
Then tells you, "The only way you can carry a baby is through
a donor egg."
Listening to the insurance company tell you,
"I'm sorry we don't cover that."
Hearing different clinics share with you the astronomical costs
it will be for it.
"It will only be around $20,000 minimum,
but don't worry it will be worth it in the end."
"Oh and by the way there are no guarantees."
So we might go around this board again,
Only they collect beyond the $200 when we pass "Go".
Sitting silently in my thoughts
Silently in wonderland
Wondering
Pondering
About the reality that exists.
The reality that I sit in.
Feeling alone
I haven't fully grieved

About the news that was given to me.
I just remained hopeful
Hoping that one day, this one day…
Will be **my** day
Will be **THE** day
That they say
"You are pregnant!"
And then a whole new journey begins.
But
Until then
I wait.
And wait.
And the longer I wait.
I sit and contemplate.
I even have conversations
About the reality that is me.
And though I enjoy shedding new light
I hope you are truly listening.
My plight may not be yours.
It probably isn't
Because our paths are different
And that's okay
Just understand that it's a sensitive area
My way is not your way
Our story may be similar
But it is
Not The Same.

*My infertility brought on many types of emotions.*
*It constantly had me in my head, mind racing, heart*
*pacing, emotional rollercoaster unending.*
*Tears would come and then they'd go.*
*I never knew when they would appear.*
*Although the tears that fell down my*
*face sometimes ceased,*
*the tears that flow through my heart continue.*

## *<u>TEARS FLOWING</u>*

I sit here in
T
E
A
R
S
Not really knowing why
All I think of is faith
And how I'm feeling inside

African American
36
Infertile
Will this baby journey ever come to term?

I believe in my heart
But there's doubts in my head
All the children I serve
Yet none that I tuck in bed.

I don't know where these

T
E
A
R
S

are flowing from
Why they came suddenly
Just the thought of the word faith
Has my mind wondering

Why do some people have kids?
Some that really don't deserve them
They treat them badly or just don't care
Yet still I sit without one of my own.

It's just not fair.
It really isn't.

I can't think of any more words
No thoughts no feelings
Just waiting on God to send me my present
My gift
My spouse
My child
My world
When will it be my turn?

I remind myself of the good that
I do.
The good that I am
But my God it gets so hard to understand.
What is my mission?
What is my purpose?
My lesson in all of this?

I know this wasn't my fault.
I cannot be blamed.
But my goodness, sometimes I do feel shame.
To be a woman and go through all of this,
To be a teacher and care so deeply feels like a nightmare in
which you wish to be pinched
These
T
E
A
R
S
keep flowing
Every now and then
I put on my face—My—smile
And push through with joy
Just hoping that one day I'll be blessed with a little girl or
boy.

May these
T
E
A
R
S
CEASE
May my mind stop wondering
May I keep believing
May I keep the faith
May love flow around me
May God grant me grace within myself
May I be surrounded by strength
May I be surrounded by love
May I be surrounded by women who will lift me up.
Because these
T
E
A
R
S
Keep
Flowing.

*My diagnosis of infertility brought on changes with
my body.*

*I couldn't understand why I had difficulty sleeping,
night sweats, migraines, brain fog, and hot
flushes unending. The changes to my mind and body
were quite embarrassing. Who wants to tell someone
about pelvic physical therapy? How do you tell
someone about vaginal pain and dryness?*
*I mean, TMI?*
*Just being transparent. These are all things that some
infertile women go through—it comes with the
infertility territory.*

*I didn't want to tell people what I was dealing with,
because at the time it didn't make any sense to me.*

*Now I know the why and to be honest—it's still hard
to share and not be embarrassed...*

# *THE TOLL*

Headaches
Hot flushes
Sleepless nights
Medication
Memory loss
Uncontrollable emotions.
Tears that fall
Back pains
Sore breasts
Not understanding why
Questioning of yourself and your mind
Wondering will any of this ever subside
Trying to fight it
Just can't seem to win
Others don't understand that it's not just growing pains that will end.
It's not just a part of life that everyone goes through
It's my reality that I'm trying to push through.

Pushing can be hard when it feels like a brick wall.
No matter how hard I try,
With all my strength and might it will not fall.

This comes with the territory of Premature Ovarian Failure. Who knew that what can sometimes feel like a punishment of no eggs could be the scrambling of everything else.

# HOT FLASHES

S
 W
  E
   A
    T

Dripping down my face.

S
 W
  E
   A
    T

Creeping up on me throughout the day.

S
 W
  E
   A
    T

Waking me up during the night.

S
 W
  E
   A
    T

I sit and do nothing

Yet you constantly show up.
I take vitamins to make you go away but
you never let up.
I pray you let me be
But I continue to see
You all over me.
S
W
E
A
T

My face
My neck My
chest at night.
I get hot then cold.
Then hot then cold.
Then hot then cold.
It's really getting old.
This game my body plays
With my body and mind
Why oh why
Can't we not play anymore
I never thought I'd be begging to actually snore.
But these sleepless nights
Are getting to me
I just want to go to dreamland
And dream a little dream
Please!

# *BARREN LAND*

Nature pours its tears onto this Earth,
I shine my sunrays upon it.

Winter comes
Still and quiet
The ground is cold
Nothing planted, nothing risen, another season of treason.

That which is beneath lies dormant
Hibernating seeds in their stubborn slumber continue to
make me wait
But I keep working to till this soil
As only the Earth can do
Praying to seed brighter days for me and for you...

My soul takes the sun and hides it nicely behind the clouds
that offer glimmers of hope.
Look at the ground,
Anything blooming?
Barren ... still.

Somnolent
Unmoving
Comatose
No more strength

I can't give in

Catatonic
Numb
My limbs still reach for Him.

As I contemplate and speculate on what wouldn't cooperate
I realize that this desolate land no longer operates and
although the seeds are stagnated
My soil is still rich
My roots are still planted
The wind I blow out from the Earth's lungs reach within
And though the seeds didn't sprout
And no blossoms bloomed
My love for life and living will forever be my fruit

## *THE HEARTBEAT OF HOPE*

*I often wondered what my child would look like, sound like, what their little personality would be. I dreamt of caring for this child, running around, being a soccer mom.*
*Doing all the family things and having all of life's conversations. Realizing that this dream may not become reality is a nightmare in itself.*
*But hope is still out there.*

# *A LETTER TO MY UNCONCEIVED...*

You are just a twinkle in my eye.
You are my hope in my doubtful days.
You are the strength that pushes me to keep smiling.
You are the joy in my saddest night.

You see the road to bring you forth hasn't been an easy
one.
I've cried and cried not knowing if you'd ever be a
possibility.
Miracles do happen right?
I had to keep believing that just around the river bend, the
flood gates would open, and you'd pour into me.

Well, that hasn't happened, yet.
I sit and wait and contemplate on the miraculous day, when
you and I would finally meet.
Me rocking back and forth and you hearing my voice as
I sing to you,
As you rest in my womb.
How did you get there?
Who cares?
Just knowing that you are with me and I am with you, and
we are one.

This journey that I'm on to find you,
To bring you forth,
Is full of bumps and bruises.
But what a ride it is.
The destination is what we celebrate.
We celebrate you.
You.
All this is for you.
So, the tears that I cried of hurt and
disappointment will one day be turned to tears of
joy.
This joy is for you.
Because you are worth it.

L
O
V
E,

Your Mommy…One Day.

# ***<u>TRADITIONS</u>***

As Christmas has come upon us, I sit and think about you.
I think about what the holidays will be like with you.
I ponder about what our traditions could/would be.
Will we go pick out a fresh tree or use an artificial one?
Will we change up the decorations each year?
Traditions.

Making gingerbread houses on Christmas Eve and baking
fresh homemade cookies will be our thing.
Listening to soulful Christmas music and of course Mariah
Carey singing her renditions.
Life will be so grand with you by my side.
Traditions.

I look forward to us watching holiday movies and drinking
hot cocoa.
We'll choose our matching pajamas to wear on Christmas
Eve and then of course our matching outfits
to slay on Christmas Day.
Waking up to the smells of homemade cinnamon rolls and
fresh cut fruit.
Watching the Macy's Day Parade.
Traditions.

Seeing the joy in your eyes as you open gifts.

Yelling at the screen as we watch football games.
Traditions.
This Christmas has been a different one, more than any
other.
Why?
Because you are on my mind.
Day and night.
Night and day.
I think of you.
I eat with you in mind.
I make decisions with you in mind.
When I see family photos of others,
It makes me wonder…
What will our photos look like?
I wonder…
Traditions.

*Imagine always wanting to join a club or organization.*
*Super excited when you feel your turn is about to come.*
*You wait and wait. Sit back and anticipate. Here it comes,*
*it's your time. But—not—quite.*
*You don't get an invitation to this club. You are not*
*included.*
*Although your heart yearns for acceptance, the reality is*
*you aren't allowed. Not allowed? What does that mean?*
*The Mom Club isn't for me?*
*To not be a part of the "Mom Club" is actually very*
*hurtful.*
*I find myself leaving rooms sometimes, just*
*because I can't take the pain of hearing the discussions*
*about the little ones from all the Moms. This is a huge*
*shock for me. The one club that I knew I'd get in.*
*The one club I knew I was absolutely qualified for.*
*The one club is the one club that*
*life*
*said*
*no.*
*Being an aunt has its perks but so does being a mom.*

## *ALWAYS AN AUNT, NEVER A MOM*

Always an aunt never a mom
Will I ever be a mom?
Will I ever get to carry my baby?
Will I ever feel you in my womb?

Always an auntie
Will I ever be a mommy?

I'm told there's always adoption.
Don't you think I know that?
I'm adopted.
Do you know the emotional attachment that was built
within me?
Always searching for that forever family.

So many options
So many choices
I know this, but why must I be limited.
So many options
So many choices
but is there?

Expensive eggs
Very few sperm

But don't forget,
"There's always adoption."
Make your choice
Hurry and choose
You're getting older now
Time is running against you.

Forget about your emotions
Forget about understanding your random thoughts.
Just focus on the positive
You have a great heart.

What good is this heart
If it can't have its own desires?
What good is this heart
If it can't feel the beat of that missing part?

The missing part that is my desire to bring life into this
world
To care for it
To cherish it
To love my very own.

So, I lie here in bed
Thinking of you
The baby I've always wanted
The child I've never seen grow up
The holidays filled with the love of you and me.

I wonder if this vision will ever be reality.
But until then
Here I am

Tears flowing down my face
Wondering if I'm worthy enough to ever see your face.
I know I didn't do anything wrong
But my goodness it does have me wondering
How can such a wonderful person have this kind of
journey?
I'm praying this isn't the end of my story.

It's not fair
It's not right
I will continue to fight.
Fight through the tears
Fight through the pain
Fight through the storms
That won't seem to go away.

Every time I turn around
Bad news comes my way.
When will doctors finally tell me something good one day.
I didn't get a fair shake
I wasn't dealt a fair hand.
I want a do over
I want life to go as I once planned.

Always an aunt, never a mom
Perhaps that's just my reality
Perhaps it's a fallacy

But if that must be my reality,

May I be the best auntie I can be.

It's not fair.
It's not right.
Why was I dealt this hand?
An aunt forever,
A mommy—Maybe never…

*I always knew I wanted to be a mom. I wanted my son or daughter to be a golfer and pilot. I wanted to open all the doors of their hearts' desires and ensure they had every opportunity to let their greatness shine.*

# *MY DREAM FOR YOU*

My dream for you is to be strong, motivated, smart and driven.
My dream for you is to have all that your heart can imagine.
I want you to play golf.
You'll be good at it.
Putt-putt will be for fun, but the golf team is where you'll be
the best.
You'll shine on the course with your putter in hand, as you
swing, you'll hit the ball, hole in one for the win!
I want you to be a pilot.
Your room will be full of planes.
You'll learn how to fly above the clouds and through the
airways.
As you explore the world, I'll be there cheering you on.
Whether you're near or far, our bond will stay strong.
These are a few dreams that I have for you.
I can't wait to see what dreams you have and watch you make
them come true.

# *TO THE CHILD I'VE ALWAYS WANTED*

How I long for the day
To hold you in my arms
To embrace you
To love you
To watch you grow.

The love that I have for you
Is so very deep
It's unexplainable
It makes me weep.

The thought of not having you
Makes me so sad.
The thought of being childless
Is a pain that I wish no one ever had
A pain that truly makes you feel helpless
To endure so much
To fight so hard
To sacrifice just to finally have you in my arms
Sometimes it feels like people just don't understand
Giving life came so easy
Some didn't want it
I'm just praying that my time will come I deserve it.
Not entitlement

I just want you here
I want you
I love you
I have so much love to share.

To the child I've always wanted
I want you to know
You are loved
You are wanted
You are in my heart
You are in my soul.
You are prayed for
I will open every door
Every door that's possible to get you here
To get you here is my heart's desire
The flame in my heart for you
I'll never extinguish that fire.

*After finding out I had Premature Ovarian Failure,
I had so many emotions. The realization of my
infertility took me on an emotional rollercoaster.
So many thoughts tap danced through my head.
A few thoughts that continued to play in my mind
were
"I don't understand why!"
and
"This isn't fair!"*

*Infertility isn't fair.
INFERTILITY ISN'T FAIR!*

# *FAIRNESS*

To make a choice is one thing
To not even have the opportunity is another.
To have the choice taken from you is beyond...
Beyond comprehension
Beyond imagination
Beyond expectations.

Wasn't my choice
Wasn't my decision
Didn't have the opportunity
It wasn't something given.

Not given the chance to say I don't want any
Not given the choice to say I do
Just one day told: A baby of your own?
Unfortunately, no, not for you.

This isn't fair
It's not right
I don't understand why me?
This isn't fair
It's not right
I'm just trying to see.

See clearly
Fully understand

The magnitude of this pain
That I can't seem to push through
Without
Feeling
shame.
Through all the tears and sleepless nights
There's got to be a way
I can't give up on this fight.
Must keep holding on and fight the urge to runaway

Fighting for a baby
Of my very own
Fighting for a baby
That I can carry and bring home.

I see so many children
As I teach them day to day
And as I pour into them
I can only imagine when it will finally be my day.

My day
My time
To pour into my child
My day
My time
To be the mother to my baby.

So, I sit
Sometimes with tears

Sometimes in deep thought
I continue to be hopeful
That one day,
That bad news will lead to another way.

Fairness is quite interesting
It can be looked at in different ways
For me fairness didn't give me a chance to go through life
any
other
way.

Infertility is serious
It's indubitably real
I just continue to pray
That fairness cuts me a deal.

*Living with the pains and hurt of this infertility*
*brought ponderings and feelings*
*I didn't realize I had.*
*It brought upon more insecurities.*
*I felt like I was less of a woman.*
*I didn't think love would ever find me.*
*I felt unpretty.*
*I would look in the mirror and just see*
*ugly infertility.*
*I have finally come to know me, understand me*
*and love me for me.*
*I am still me.*
*I am still a beautiful woman.*
*I am not my infertility.*
*I am not my infertility.*

*I AM NOT MY INFERTILITY.*

# *<u>I AM WOMAN: BEYOND INFERTILITY,<br>NOT DEFINED BY IT</u>*

My day darkened when I discovered my infertility.
Had NO idea that THESE hips would betray me.
I never realized how much that one discovery would
define me.

I explored my thoughts and feelings
Battled with emotions imploding from within me
No clue of what the beginning was or even the end.

How I questioned myself
My existence
Wondering if I'd ever heal

No longer feeling like a woman
More like less than,
Ugly and with no sex appeal.
This wasn't part of the plan!
THIS WASN'T part of the plan!

NEVER thought I'd no longer
Like me
Love me
BE ME!

Couldn't look in the mirror without bawling
Caribbean rains fell from these brown eyes that no longer were
filled with hope.

WHO WAS this person?
This "woman" with no eggs?

Body…barren
Soul…lifeless

What man would want me now?
I mean seriously
Hormonal issues that made me sigh
Weight gain
Body pains
Need I go on?
THIS life of infertility brought me early menopause.

I couldn't understand why! WHY?!

Still question it to this day
Why I had to be chosen
To go through life this way

It took a long time,
Years actually
For me
To finally see me
The one He created me to be

Sure, I have moments of doubt
They come and go
But what's certain and true is
I am strong, powerful, bold
Resilient, intelligent, courageous, uncontrolled.
A natural beauty to behold.

I
WOULD'VE BEEN AN EXCELLENT MOTHER.

And even though my day darkened when I discovered my
infertility
I was woman then
And I can confidently say
I
AM
WOMAN NOW!

# *ECHOES OF THE MIND*

*Infertility is a lonely club to be in. The topic of infertility has been so quietly kept, therefore you don't even realize that others are in this lonely club too. But how can it be a "club" with so much sadness? Nothing to party about, sing to, laugh and dance about. The toll of infertility, the waves of emotions that it brings, the nonstop thoughts that run through your head, the inner feelings that you think no one will ever understand...all coupled with desolation and emptiness...These things, unfortunately, all work together to bring gray clouds, dark skies—utter despair.*

## *IT*

You don't really know what someone else is going through
In the middle of any day or night IT creeps up on you.

You can't shake IT.
You don't know what to do.
IT takes hold of you IT
changes you.
IT walks and talks just like you.
But IT's NOT you.

You stop eating
You eat too much
Your bank account starts depleting.

IT's got you clouded
You can't see.
Is IT you?
Is IT reality?
OR
Is IT this thing?
This thing that won't go away.
The thing that haunts you throughout the day.
IT keeps you up at night
And when you finally sleep
IT suffocates you in your dreams.

You can't figure out what's wrong with you.
You just need a lot more of ME
And a lot less of you.

This YOU is who YOU don't know very well.
Yet let IT tell you
And you'd think everything was swell.
As if this is how IT's supposed to be.
More of IT and less of me.

But I'm tired now.

Tired of IT all in my head
Tired of sleepless nights and not making nice with my bed.
Tired of the weight gain and the negative thoughts Tired of the
migraines and all that I've lost.

Lost MYself, MY joy, MY passion for life.
Lost MY humor, MY zest, MY quality of life.

I can't imagine ME—Myself—I
Anymore.
I just pray that she comes through and opens a door.
A door to ME, to love, to happiness
A door to hope, to joy, to who I sincerely miss
The ME—The person—The one who I cherish.

You see this thing that creeps up on you
Is so ugly and mean
IT's deceptive and alarming

And sometimes IT is difficult to see.

But once YOU see IT
You'll know for certainty what IT is
IT's NOT YOU IT's NOT who
IT wants YOU to believe IT is.

It's this thing that blinds you.
And takes you off your balance
IT makes YOU believe things about YOUR self
That is completely fictitious

This thing they call depression Is like a deep
sadness—in ugly form.
I no longer wanna sit in IT.
I no longer wanna walk in IT.
I gotta get out of IT.
IT is NOT ME
IT can't be me anymore.

You are strong.
You are bold.
You are beautiful.

You are radiant.
You are loved.
You are treasured.
Your talent is unmeasured.

You are caring and graceful.
Your intentions are true, and your heart is pure.
You are intelligent and patient
Wise beyond your years, mature.

You boldly speak up for others
You stand up for what is right.
No matter the situation, you carry His light.

It's time to take a stand.
YOU stand up and IT stands down
No longer will you be defeated by this IT cloud

I can't deal with IT anymore.
Gotta get out
Gotta get back
Gotta put ME back in order.

Heaviness no more
Sadness no more
Overeating no more
Spending no more.

Bring on the happiness
Bring on the joy.
Bring on the love for myself
That I once had before.

No more self-doubt
No more negative thoughts
Work out the body
Work out the mind
Bring me back stronger than before.

Gather my circle
Gather my tribe
Gather all the healthy habits that brought ME back to life.
I gotta keep pushing
I gotta get strong
Life is greater
Knowing I belong.
There IS greater purpose
There IS greater love
There IS meaning for ME and YOU from above.

# *HIDE AND SEEK*

What's wrong with me you ask
What's wrong?
Well, quite a bit of things
But you'd only really know this if you truly wanted to know
me.

You see I have trust issues
I let people in
and then those same people I let out
I keep being reminded that I can't call everyone a friend.

I'm a great person
I'm truly an awesome friend
The only way you'd know this is
if you knew how to be one too.

Friends.
How many of us have them?
Friends.
Ones you can depend on.

Friends.
Men, I'm a little hip to the game on
But friends,
Now that's one that I'm not wise on

Because even with my trust issues,

I still desire that friendship,

That sisterhood,
That depend on me and I know I can depend on you
True loyalty type of thing

I get high hopes about that friendship thing
Not realizing that
Perhaps
The only real friend in this "friendship"
Was—Me

So, I rely on myself
I deal with my internal issues
I cry it out and then put on a smile and go on about my way
To a place that causes me to hibernate
Away from the world
Away from reality
Away from me

These moments don't last for a long time
But when they come,
I sure wish I had a friend,
Who I could confide in
That friend to share my sorrows with…
Talk about them, cry it out, laugh away the rains from my face
Then take those same pains

Run
Hide
And never
Seek them again.

# *UNWANTED FRIEND*

I feel you creeping up on me.
My heart races
My mind is pacing
Words get lost
Words run together
I literally can't see through the stormy clouds of you.

I try to calm you down and bring some peace to you
But for some reason the stresses of life are what you cling to.
You won't let me go
You've made a home in my head
And from there you've tap danced through my body and led.

Led my mind
Took the lead
Decided this is where you'd like to be.

This rollercoaster of emotions,
That you ride through my body
Only brings about pain and doubt.

It keeps going and going
When will it end?

It's the image of Sonic zooming around and around a golden
ring
That never bends.
Feeling like it won't stop until after it reaches that super speed,

But it doesn't feel like a superpower,
No, it's my Achilles heel
My kryptonite indeed.

It's a mystery that I can't solve
No clues to the end
I don't win a prize
It's like an unwanted best friend.

It won't leave me alone
It just keeps bothering me
I beg in my heart,
Please just leave.

Anxiety isn't wanted
I never asked for it actually
It just showed up one day and said, "I'm here!
Better get used to me!"
It's bothersome and quarrelsome
and causes chaos in my brain.
My body feels it
My sweat displays it
The damage that it brings causes pain.

So I fight this inner guy
Each day and night
Breathing
Positive thinking
Praying

And believing
With the help of God,
I can quiet this unwanted friend down.
And prayerfully I pray, it won't stay around.

# ***TIRED***

I am sooooooo tired.
Tired of ALL of this.
The doctor's results.
THIS body.
My insecurities.

Tired of self-doubt.
Tired of being there for others,
But for me…no one is around.

Tired of dreaming.
of hoping. of lack of understanding.
Tired of lack of empathy.
Tired.

Tired of the unknown. of not knowing.
Tired of uncertainties.
Tired of curiosities.
Tired of trying. of crying.
Tired of
Just
Being Me.
Tired.

# ***BEHIND THESE EYES***

The enigmatic mask that I wear suppresses the weight of
despair
My ancestors
My era
The future of my people

The torrential rains that fall from these eyes of the hidden
Exposes the truth and oppressive history that I live in

Behind these eyes are hope, strength and resilience
Encouraging and empowering the next generation.
My soul reaches up high for the lives that have been taken.

Behind these eyes lies a tornado of emotions,
I quickly turn my head so no one can see my expressions.
The hole in my sky casts a shadow on the side of my face that
is concealed for I cannot reveal the treacherous hurt that won't
seem to heal.

So I stare out at you, the world, and back at me.
Contemplating whether or not the real me will be
recognized
Behind these eyes.

## *ME FIRST*

Choosing me first feels like a mystery
A fallacy
A tragedy
That I would be
Choosing me

Choosing me
My thoughts
My feelings
My wants, hopes, and dreams

Being authentically me
To the point that even
I
See
Me

You see I've gone so long without seeing me
Not recognizing me
Not acknowledging me
Not knowing,
Me

I was so concerned with you
And others
Their thoughts
Their feelings
What works for them
Yet never thinking about what works for…
Me.

A living lie
Because
I
Chose to focus on others
And faltered on parts
Of
Me.

I wore a smile
Batted my eyes
Sucked up the tears when I wanted to cry.
I,
Pushed back my true thoughts and feelings and,
Disguised it with,
"Whatever you wants"
And
"Whatever you thinks"
And
"What works for you is fine with me"
Yet never truly putting Me first.

Answering questions with what I think you'd think is correct
Sharing thoughts of what I thought you'd prefer me to think.


Holding back feelings scared that what I really feel might
make you feel differently about me.


Me.
Authentically me.
How am I to be authentically me?
No part to play.
No line to say.
No feelings to feel.
Just—Be—Me.


You see,
I've played me for so long,
This version of me,
That prefers to, people please
To hope that, others hang on
Hang on to me
And not let go
Not walk away
Just enjoy the show


You see, the show that I've been playing
The cast keeps changing
And while I continue to play Me

Why do I somehow end up alone?
I've done my part
I thought I did
I smiled
I listened
I nodded and agreed with them.
Yet, still I sit
Trying to identify
What I,
The one, I played,
Did wrong…
What did I miss?

It's difficult playing Me
Trying to be the Me that others want Me to be
The Me that isn't focused on Me
The Me that focused on being the versions of me that others
see.

Me,
First,
That's a challenging concept
One that I must accept
If I want to be my best
self—ME.

# *<u>WHO CARES</u>*

Self-care
Mind care
Body care
I
Care
You
Care
We
Care.

Care.

Care for you
Care for me
Care for families

But do we
Really Care?

When someone asks,
"How are you feeling?"
Do we really want to hear?
Do we really want to care?

Because if I truly listened
If I wanted to hear
My care would be

Your care
And his care
Would be her care.

Do all cares look the same?
Is the response that comes next
the one that we expect?
Is it the answer that we already have drummed up in our
heads?

Are our answers robotic?
Already programmed in us?
So when we want to share
We can't
Because the answer isn't in us.

We're compute
Programmed
Bit by bit
And byte by byte
That we can't even understand
The human complexities
The innate true feelings
The matters of the heart

That has people hurting inside
But smiling from afar.

You wouldn't know it
Unless you knew them
Because you'd try to take them apart
Piece by piece
Part by part
Attempting to mend broken hearts.

Brokenness is a thing
A thing we don't talk about much
We sometimes are too busy
That we can't focus on such.

So I ask again,
Do we really care?
Do we know how to care?
Do we even dare?

Dare to step away from the programming
Put it away
Box it up
Ship it out
Let the realness play
Let it share Let it show
Let it tell you how
How it feels

How it's doing
Let the true feelings appear.

You see this type of care
Puts care on a platform
It highlights and spotlights
It shows "care" off
The importance of care
Seems too hard to believe
If we take it
And hold it
To high esteem.
Care has its own way of doing things
It shows up
Shows out
Makes one truly feel it
Making one feel heard
Noticed
And appreciated.

If no one has asked you
If no one has told you
If no one has shared
How are YOU really feeling?
I really do care.

# *EMOTIONS*

Happiness
Sunshine
Butterflies
Openness

Kindness
Warmth
Flowers
Brightness

Tranquility
Rainbows
Lakes
Visibility

Oceans
Sun showers
Joyful music
Emotions

Emotions can be felt
Emotions can be seen
Emotions can reveal a lot about you and me

Emotions can take you high
Emotions can bring you down low

Emotions travel with you wherever you go.

How you choose to express them
Is really up to you
Just be careful how you choose to use them
Don't let them convolute
Convolute the truth
Convolute the facts
Convolute what's before you

May they not uproot
Uproot you from reality
What truly exists

You see, emotions can sometimes take you through
rollercoasters and twists.
Twist you up
Twist you down
Twist you around and around

Until the bliss you once had now ceases to resist
Resists the conflicts of your emotions
That constricts you from growing
Causing pain to be inflicted
Instead of
Changing the script and
Taking control and consoling
What feelings are being felt

Letting go
Breathing in
Blowing them all out
Bringing you back to center
Now,
What was this truly all about?

# *<u>SONGS OF THE HEART</u>*
## *<u>UNFOLDING</u>*

# *DEAR YOU*

Dear you,

Wow, it feels like forever since we last had a true heart to
heart.

I'm sorry I haven't sat you down and shared this with you
from the start.

First, let me begin by saying I love you.
I know that's sometimes difficult to hear.
And then again,
It's not said enough.
So let me tell you again,
I love you.
If you don't ever hear it from anyone else,
Know for certainty that
I love you.

I love you for who you are
I love the way your eyes sparkle like night stars
I love the way you treat others
I love the purity of your heart.
I love your kind gestures
Always willing to help someone else
I love the way you shine as you walk into any space.
I love the way I can count on you,
You'll always be my ace.

I love the time we spend together
I love how you take care of me.
Lately, you've started making me a priority.
Thank you for that.
I appreciate it.
It means a lot to me.

I love your brain,
The way you think
How you debate back and forth and look at all angles
Before your decision is complete.
I love the way you talk things out
How you speak so eloquently
I love your nerdy side
How that thesaurus is your bestie
And the dictionary is your sidekick.
I love how you write it out
You're so emotionally intelligent.

If I didn't get to know you before
I'm so glad I know you now
Who you are
What you bring to this world
His purpose for you is immeasurable
I don't doubt.

So as my love letter to you

Comes to an end

I want you to know that I will always be here for you
As your confidant and friend.

Forgive me for not loving you first
Because that's what we all must do
Love yourself
Love me
I most certainly do.

So next time we chat it won't seem like forever
And it won't take a letter
For me to say,

Self,
I love you sweet lady
You'll forever be my number one, my queen.

*I think of myself as a simple girl in this crazy world*
*who likes the simple things.*
*Words, laughter, music, food, travel, and*
*adventures!*

# *LOVE LANGUAGE*

What's your love language?
I'm asked.
What's my love language?
It's easy to describe
Yet hard to maintain
Not for me,
But for others
I guess that's what they say.

More like that's what they show
Because their words say one thing
But their actions speak differently

My love language is simple, you see.
Show kindness
Be patient
Soft words
Thoughtful gestures
Effective communication
Consistency
Loyalty and trust beyond measure

Intelligence
Laughter
Thrift store treasures
Love kids
Love travel
Cooking and dancing together are a joy and a pleasure.

Dad jokes
Game nights
Family time fun
Long talks
Long walks
Enjoy the rising and setting of the sun.

Simplicity
Honesty
Transparency too.
Learning together
Growing together
Sharing a love I never knew.

What's my love language?
It's simple you see
Just
love me
for me.

## *DETOUR*

"First comes love, then comes marriage, then comes the
baby in the baby carriage…"

That's what I always thought.
But for me, that's not how the song ends up being played.
Amid my struggles with infertility, I didn't realize
infidelity was knocking on my door.
The man who I thought I'd be spending the rest of my life
with,
The man who I thought I'd be creating a baby with, Was
a wolf in sheep's clothing.
When his true self came out,
I had two choices,
Stay and ignore the red flags or leave and start over.
I chose to get off of Denial Drive and take a right turn up
Hope Highway.
I had no idea of where it would lead, but I knew happiness
had to be on the horizon.

# *DEBRIS*

Emotionally I'm not strong,
I'm weak.
Tears keep falling from my face,
You used me.
I let you.
How?
I ignored the red flags that were in my face.
You never cared about me.
You loved me, because you needed me.
So now I sit here
In tears.
Not upset or hurt by us being over
Mad at myself for being so stupid
Stupid for loving you.
Stupid for thinking you actually loved me.
I built my credit up before you.
And I let you crumble it down.
I can't even get a car loan now.
Going into bankruptcy at the age of 36.
You made my credit sick.
You make me sick.
Sick of you.
Literally sick.
Headaches, migraines, nausea
Sick.

So I contemplate
About all the times we spent
It came and went
Like a spiraling roller coaster going up and down and
round and round.
These tears that fall are not because you were so great.
They fall because
Because
Because
You see before there is an effect there is a cause
You were the cause…
The cause…
The cause of…
My hurt and pain
My credit dropping
My confidence fading
My smile ceasing
My tears falling.
You were the cause of…
My negative energy
My insecurities.
You brought all of that to my table.
And now I must sit
Alone
At my table
And figure out what I am to do
With the leftovers.

*Starting over can be scary and nerve wrecking---*
*but taking that step towards new beginnings,*
*letting go of*
*whatever and whoever doesn't bring your world*
*peace, that's what erases the fright and doubt.*
*Choosing me*
*when not feeling valued in any type of relationship*
*has always been the best decision...*
*---and sometimes the journey requires just that,*
*no one else,*
*just---you.*

# ***STARTING OVER***

Starting over isn't an easy journey.
I lie awake early in the morning.
I toss and turn all night long.
I have bad dreams and see images of my past.
The past that hurt me.
The past that brought me to this
point.
The past that channeled negativity, low confidence and
despair.
How do I start over when I still feel this ugliness inside?
How do I start over when I am mad at myself for allowing
myself to be used?
How do I start over when I feel like there's no place to go?
How do I start over when I don't even know
how—-to— start?
Starting over.

I question myself all the time with the whys, what
happened, didn't you see the red flags?
I am naturally hard on myself, but with this…
I'm even harder.
I have a Master's degree.
I was going places.
Why did I have to fall for toxicity
hidden under a mask of love?

Love?
Certainly not real love.
No way it could've been.
Love wouldn't hurt this badly.
Starting over.
A new day.
A new life.
Fresh air.
Fresh start.
But is it?  How can you start over when the past is still
lingering?
How can you start over when images still reside in your
phone and in your head?
Years of a false reality.
A play by play of what once was.
A play by play of what you looked past.
A play by play of what you allowed.
Is all of this part of my "starting
over"?
Was it better to live in a false
reality?
Were those play by plays better than the misery that I'm
currently feeling?
This, is my new start.
Perhaps misery isn't the right word, but it's unequivocally
loneliness.
I feel like I left one false reality to play in a pretentious
one.

I'm pretending that life is so much better, but clearly, in
this moment, I don't feel that way.
On one hand it is.
I mean living in toxicity is no way to truly live.

On the other hand, living in a maze where your mind keeps
bringing you to dead ends of your past isn't a way to live
either.

Perhaps that's the key word.
"Dead"
The life of toxicity…dead.
The days of using me…dead.
The days of low standards meets low expectations…dead.
The days of settling…dead.
Dead.

Death is a hard idea to come to grips with.
When something is dead it no longer exists.
It no longer endures pain or
suffering.
At the same time, it can no longer bring about pain or
suffering.
It's gone and only its memories
linger.
So with this thought, what else can death bring?
Death can bring peace, solitude and sometimes closure.
Death can bring forth new points of view.

Death can also bring forth life and new ways of living.
Stay with me.
Death is super hard to deal with
But it also reminds me of how important it is to laugh.
The importance of living.
The death of someone is beyond hard. The death of
something, or in this case a relationship is hard too.
But in both cases, we can learn, and we can channel our
energy to decide where we go from here.
For me, I'm still figuring it out.
I'm choosing the road that leads to a strong, confident, and
happy me.
I feel like I'm taking baby steps down this road though.
I mean I feel like I'm moving at turtle speed, nope make
that snail speed.
But at least I'm moving right?
I once read a quote that said, "It feels good to be lost in the
right direction."
That my friends, is definitely how I'm feeling.
So I go back to one of my original questions:
Was it better to live in a false reality?
Nope it's better for me to be lost but heading in the right
direction.
Solitude, peace, happiness, serenity, joy, laughter,
gratitude, and love will all be there to greet me…perhaps
along the way or at the end.
I'm absolutely looking forward to meeting them as I create
my new reality, a new me, a new start.
Starting over.

# *ME 2.0*

A better version of me.
You think you know me.
You thought you knew me.
Just wait until you see me.

Like immense pressure under the ashes This
diamond will appear.
Not to be confused by the rubble that was once around me.
A diamond in the rough.
Elevation is coming.
I will rise up.
Can't stay down for too long.
Because like the diamond
I maintain my strength
Even when heat and pressure is upon me
I keep shining.
No amount of negativity can stop me from shimmering.

You wanted me down.
You counted me out.
Heck even I began to doubt.
Doubted myself and my purpose
Doubted me being without.

Without you.
You who my life began to be about.
My light slowly began to flicker.
My glow slowly began to vanish.

But no more.

The sunny days are shining.
The smile is illuminating.
Dark clouds have moved on.
Brighter days are coming.

Coming my way is happiness.
On the horizon is a rainbow.
Soon approaching is true love.
And finally, I see you out of my way.
It's a new day.

So, This,
This diamond in the rough is
standing strong, hard and tough.
Shining through the rubble of pain, fear, and doubt.
Elevating above the negativity.
Seeing beyond the worries.
Rising above the ashes of the past.

What we had was artificial, synthetic, phony, and fake.
I believed in it wholeheartedly and that was my mistake.
You see, a wolf in sheep's clothing can only keep his tail
covered for so long.
A cubic zirconia can only imitate
And never duplicate
The real thing.
That which is me.
I will keep sparkling
Because
This diamond is forever.

# *WHAT HAPPENED?*

I'm so confused
Perhaps it's me
That MUST be it,
Something is wrong with me

You meet someone,
You state your intentions, and they state theirs.
Simple.
At least it seems that way.

What happened to: Do you like me?
Circle yes or no

What happened to courtship?
What happened to going steady?
What happened to monogamy?
What happened to being straight up and honest?

Like in the words of Paula Abdul,
"Straight up now tell me is it gonna be you and me forever?
Oh oh oh!"
You know?

What happened to "first comes love then comes marriage
then comes baby in the baby carriage"?

What happened to really getting to know folks?

Why does a conversation with me lead to you thinking that
I want to Netflix and chill, "chill?"

Why does me being me, which is as sweet as can be might
I add, make you think
I'm a "challenge" that you must conquer?

Why do the words, "I'm a relationship girl" make you
think something contrary to what was stated?

You stated your intentions, I stated mine.
For some strange reason, I thought they aligned.

But slowly and surely, the truth came out
Your actions, not your words, showed what you were truly
about.

So, for the record,
Hi, my name is Melissa.
I'm not looking to hook up,
No, I don't want to "chill"
There's more to me than physical appeal.

I have a Master's degree,
A teacher of 12 years

Head raised high and so are my standards
Please believe, What I ask for I can also deliver.

I'm looking for a king who can complement this queen
One to travel with, explore the world, adventures and
laughter on repeat.
I'm certainly not complicated,
Quite simple as can be
Just hoping for the man that will walk beside me.

BUT what I am NOT about,
Is wasting time and energy
That, I certainly don't have any to give out.
So, I don't know what happened
And I don't know why you would try
For something you not only aren't ready for but will also
quickly be denied.
But the next time you think you can waste my time…
Please Just
Don't.

*Where art thou—the side from whence my rib came. I look forward to the kind of love that He has for me.*
*I look forward to love finding me.*
*I believe, I hope, I have faith…*
*from my heart's desires to your ears Lord…*

# TO BE...

To be wanted
To be desired
To be chosen
To be heard.

To be felt
To be cherished
To be loved
To be put first.

To be held
To be honored
To be cared for
To be reassured

To be valued
To be appreciated
To be seen
To be supported.

To be treasured
To be embraced
To be understood
To be affirmed

To share adventures
To have fun
To grow individually
To grow together
To make lasting memories
To share special code words
To see what life has to discover

To be
To share
To have
To make
Here's to love
Here's to hope
Here's to no more heartbreak

To you
To me
To what could be
Endless joy
Endless happiness
Endless possibilities.

*I'm a 90s R&B kind of girl.*
*I still believe in love and happily ever*
*after. I pray for my future husband and*
*pray he finds me.*
*I've been asked what I look for in a*
*potential mate...*
*I hope he's all this and more.*

# *<u>SOMEONE</u>*

I…. need…. someone…

Someone…. who enjoys laughter…
but…doesn't see me as a punchline.
Someone…who…openly…communicates…
and…isn't…close minded.
Someone…who…brightens…my…day…
without…bringing shade.

Someone…

Someone…who…understands…that…chivalry…
illuminates me…and…
Keeps the possibility…of romance…alive.
Someone…who…enjoys traveling…lives life freely…and
knows…how to…
Just…have…fun.

Someone.

Someone…who is…honest…and wise…
Who loves… being…by my side…
Someone…who…likes game nights…but…isn't a player.

Someone…who…believes in a…never ending…
happily ever after…old skool kind of love…
Someone…who…tries…new
things…and…enjoys…making…memories.

Where…are…you…someone?

Someone

Someone…who…takes our selfies…and is…selfless…
Someone…who…cooks…up…peace…
and…leaves drama…out…the recipe.
Someone…who…paints our canvas…with all our
adventures…

What awaits us on these new horizons?

Someone.

Someone…who…enjoys…Looney Tunes,
but…. puts kid games…behind him.
Someone…who…has the heart of a dove
Yet…protects…like an elephant
Someone…who…holds family near….
and values…. commitment.

Someone.

Someone who…loves…a Claire Huxtable…
with a side of…Janet and…a sprinkle…of Cardi B.
Someone who isn't…afraid to be….
transparently…him…and is proud…
to have…me…be…me.

I….need…. someone…
I…. want…someone…
Someone……who is…. uniquely……you.

Someone…. who……loves…. all…. of….me

# *HIM*

He will see me
He will know it's me.
He will communicate with me.
He will embrace me.

He will trust me
He will want me
He will honor me

He will believe in me.
He will pray for me
He will pray with me.

He will lead me.
He will guide me
He will stick beside me.

He will include me
He will not want to lose me.
He will compliment me
He will date me.

He will understand me
He will choose me
He will be my best friend
My forever confidant.

He will be my peace.
He will be my king.
He will pursue me.
He will woo me.
He will make me a priority.
He will show me that he needs me.

He will appreciate me.
Appreciate my quirkiness
Appreciate my nerdiness
Appreciate my kindness
Appreciate my dad jokes

Appreciate my mind.
Appreciate my heart
Appreciate the love that I possess inside.
Appreciate my beauty
Appreciate my flaws
Appreciate me all in all.

When he shows up
He will see me
And I will see him. I won't have to
chase him Freely take off my mask.
He will understand me and embrace my past.
The PTSD of trials and errors of relationships
Won't change his view of me.
He will be consistent

He will be patient
He will be trusting

He will remind me it's okay to let go.
Let go of distrust
Let go of the past
Let go of what was not meant to last.

Let go and Let God
Lead you into a new beginning
A beginning of love
A beginning of trust
A beginning with
Him
Me
Us.

So, I await that day
Await that moment
Await his arrival

I look forward
To meeting him
To embracing him
To spending forever
With…him.

# *THE GAMES WE PLAYED*

Roses are red
Violets are blue
Wait, is that how this goes?
Is love really true?

Let's try this again
Roses are red
Violets are blue
Guess Who?
You finally found me and I found
you

Where were you hiding?
Behind the swing sets?
Playing Lego's?
Fighting bad guys?
Building a Barbie Dream Home for me?

I called you over when we played Red Rover,
but you were too busy playing Checkers to notice
me when I yelled for you to come over.

There you were standing in Four Squares,
When I asked you to put down the Marbles and
help me with that Jump Rope,

Do you Dare?


We Double-Dutched, but you had cooties!
Ewww don't touch!
It would've been too much of a fuss to trust you Hiding
and Seeking me and not lust.

I paid attention and stopped,
Red Light!
Until it was finally our turn,
Green Light!
We Hopscotched to see what Simon Says
and Duck Duck Goosed our way
to have a seat in our Musical Chairs.
I had to Tag you in only,
so you'd finally Capture The Flag
and ultimately capture my heart for the win.

# *LA FLEUR*

I feel gray
Chest pains
Why?
Hurt
Confused
Will my skies ever be blue?
I live in this garden all alone
Yet still surrounded by other beautiful flowers
Look! Here they come
It's time to choose
Oh good!
Yay for you!
Okay certainly it will be me next
Oh that one is a good one!
So glad you saw that one!
Oh look! Here comes another one!
Surely, it's mine
Nope not this time.
I sit again looking around
Realizing that I'm still attached to this ground
Not picked up
Not picked out
Not chosen once again.
Each time they come I sit with hope and adoration
I continue to smile

I bask in the sunlight
Only for night fall to come
And it's just me and the moonlight
When will I be selected?
Can't they smell this sweet nectar?
Why do they continue to walk by this unique and one-of-a-
kind treasure?
Sure, I've been through some things
Only a couple of toxic bees
But still I grew stronger
Stood taller
And became unapologetically me
But for some reason
They either walk by
Or they stop by
Take a glance
Even leave me thinking
That perhaps they'll come back

Pick me up and hold me near
Or perhaps as some birds chirped
It's just not my season.
I get that but
Gee whiz when will it ever be?

# *HEY YOU!*

Hey!...You!…
Yeah…you…
The one…. sitting…right…. over…there…
I…. want you….to know that…
I see you… I…. see…. you.

I see the way…you…move…
I see…how you…. interact.
I see…that…. gorgeous…smile
And those…mmmm…captivating…. eyes.

I notice…how…you…speak…
How you…. quietly…make an entrance…
I notice…. how…. your head bobs…
As you…. sit back…and…. listen.

I…watch…how you…. show…empathy.
How you…take…time…to…understand.
How you…. show up…. for others….
as their…biggest fan…

You…seem…. sooo…. quiet
Yet…. when given…a platform….
about your…. passion…
OH…you've got A LOT to say….

Keep sharing your mission.


The way......you.... thoughtfully...express.... your mind.
The way.... you let...your.... creativity...shine.

How you...speak into others...when everyone can't...
How you.... are...always.... willing...to take.... a chance.
Take a chance...on...love
Take a chance...on....me
Shooting your shot...
Possibly...missing...
But don't...miss this...opportunity
You can.... always.... bet...on...me.

# *SUNNY DAYS*

Love is like a sunny day
Beautiful, bright and ready to play
It's warm and inviting
The heat of its passion
The sun's shine dries
The rains that once fell from these eyes
For someone who wasn't even worth a cloudy day
Feel the breeze from the trees
As you speak through the wind
The sweat that drips from every ounce of work
that you put in
To make THIS work
To show your true commitment
The mood of a sunny day is like your love
Calm, playful, easy breezy and real
The way a sunny day can only make you feel
Oh, how I love sunny days
And although I haven't experienced love
I sure do hope to experience it
in
this
way.

# *WHEN I SEE YOU...*

When I see you
WHEN...I...SEE...YOU
I see...the strength....... of a lion...
The...confidence......of an eagle...
The...fearlessness...of a wolf...
The...physique...of a stallion...
The...growth...of a lotus flower...
I see...the color...green...representing...your...healing

When I see you...
I see that...First Corinthians love...
You know that...ruby...red...flame...of passion...
I see a butterfly...soaring...to new heights...far above...

When I SEE YOU...
I see the POWER of a BLACK...PANTHER...
I see the...heaviness...of a cloud...
YET the
OPENNESS...that...allows...
EMOTIONS...to...pour...out

When I.... SEE.... YOU...
I see.... hope...for the future...
I see.... the BATTLE SCARS...of LIFE....
Blown limbs....

But I also see…

The FOUNDATION……. of your soul…
And the…. UNWAVERING…roots…from within…
that STEM…from…Him.
Mmmm When I see you…
I see…. sunshine…and…brighter days…
Feel your joy…and…
See the laughter…written all…over...your face.

When I see you

Mmmmm When I SEE YOU
I see NO…ONE…ELSE…
It ALL just…disappears…
Rains…cease…
Dark skies…become…bright
No more strifes…no more fights…
Juuust…sweet…melodies… Jazzy…conversations…
And…90's R&B…playful banter.

Real talks……long walks…….
Quiet moments………soft touches…….
Peaceful breezes…….unending teasing…….

You……    Me…….
When I see you…mmm…mmmm…mmmm…
When I SEE YOU….

When
I
SEE
YOU…
I... see….US

# *<u>I LOVE YOU</u>*

Whyyyyy
Does my heart yearn for you
To know you
To be close to you
To hear from you

Your laugh makes me smile
Your smile brings me warmth
Your warmth spreads to others as you eagerly serve.

Your eyes speak to my heart
Your words are music to my ears
Your ears are always available to listen Making sure
everyone is heard.

I enjoy you.
I enjoy being one with you.
Spending time with you
Whether it's on a movie date, having dinner, or just
watching tv.
Alone time with you is splendid as can be.

Thinking things through
Talking things out
Rereading your writing

Taking all the positives in and blowing the rest out.

You are absolutely amazing.
A pulchritudinous sight to see
Your brains, beauty, kindness towards others and empathy.

You crack me up with your corny jokes You make
me smile with your knowledge. The way you
strive to make memories is absolutely
acknowledged.

I love the way you plan outings
New adventures are always on the horizon.
You're good for always making sure everyone is jiving.

You are one of a kind
Simply a rare treasure that's true
Your peaceful spirit
And compassionate nature
Is what draws others to
you.

On stormy days,
You calm me
And bring me back to center
No matter what I'm going through
You remind me He is the author and finisher.

I don't know what I'd do without you

You are my everything
I'm so thankful for that day
When I finally fell in love with you
I knew
It was forever meant to be.

No one sees you like I see you
I'm so glad I not only see but believe
You are greatness.
You are boldness.
You are confidence.
You are love
You are me
And I love you for being you
I love you for being me.

Real love
Complete love
Self-love

# *THE VOICE RISING*

# *WHO AM I?*

Let me introduce myself to you.
Kind
Sweet
Honest
Friendly
Loyal
Peaceful
A voice for the voiceless
Intelligent
Caring
Shy
Dependable
Creative
Polite
Funny
A wonderful lady to meet.

There's so much to learn about me
There's so much that I like to do
Traveling
Trying new foods
Comedy shows
Musicals

Broadway plays
Disney movies
Education
Live music
Cultures
Salsa dancing
Reading books too.

Have I been through a lot?
Of course, who hasn't?
Trauma
Cheaters
Liars
Deceivers
Fakes
Phonies
Not the ones-ies.

Has that scarred me?
Perhaps, but not really.
Do I still believe in love?
Oh absolutely!
I believe love will find me
And he'll find his way to me
He'll see past my insecurities.
He'll secure my heart Protecting it and nurturing it
From the start.

What's my problem?
The waiting process
When will it be my turn?
I'm 41
Single
Childless
Waiting for happily ever after.
Does it exist?
Will it be a reality for me?
Yes indeed. I do believe.

Do I have flaws?
Of course. I mean I can't be that great.
I overthink.
Overanalyze
I'm my biggest critic.

I'm a cheerleader for others but can be hard on myself.
I don't give myself enough grace or enough credit.
I sometimes don't see,
What others see in me.
Both on the outside and inside
The beauty that He has given me.

So, who I am
Is what I've been through.
Who I am

Is who I choose to be

Remaining the me that He has created me to be.
Loving
Joyful
Peaceful
Patient
Kind and good
Faithful
Gentle
Generous
Friendly
Like The Little Engine that Could
I keep going and going
No matter the obstacles
Pushing forward
Persevering
Not letting anything or anyone stop me.

So again, I say to you my friends
Let me introduce myself to you
This
Is
Me.

*I have always had my own insecurities.
Infertility heightened and brought upon a few
more of these.*

*I no longer felt good enough and often had
feelings of inadequacies of being a woman.
I didn't think I was enough.*

*Through therapy and tapping into my gift of
writing, I learned how to navigate through my
emotions and began the healing process in a
positive and productive way*

*.
I can now confidently say,*

*I AM ENOUGH.*

*YOU ARE also ENOUGH.*

# *I AM ENOUGH*

Not good enough
Not smart enough
Not pretty enough
Not wise enough

Not bold enough
Not strong enough
Not decisive enough
Not loud enough

Not fat enough
Not thin enough
Not fine enough
Not light enough

Not dark enough
Not tall enough
Not this enough
Not that enough
Not enough
Not enough
Not enough

ENOUGH IS ENOUGH

Enough with the downgrading,

---the naysaying,
---the excuses
Enough with the lies that we tell ourselves
Enough with the negativity and the noise
Enough with listening to that piercing voice

Enough with the mind tricking
Enough with the mind gaming
Enough with the sabotaging
Enough with it all No more.

No more
Sabotaging ourselves our families
our dreams
And
Who we are supposed to be.

No more
Sabotaging our relationships our jobs
Sabotaging the love that was meant for me.

For me
For you
For us
For Him

To give Him glory
To be the salt
To light up the world with His story.

If I am in Him
And He is in me
If I am from Him
And He made me from He
Then I am the light
I am full of flavor
I AM ENOUGH
And so is my neighbor.

You see we are He
And He is us
Therefore, WE will ALWAYS be ENOUGH.

So shut the doors to the lies and deceit
Close your ears to what ISN'T meant for you and me.

Enough is enough.
We are all that
He created us in His image
That's a fact.

So chin up
Head raised high
Enough
Is
Enough
We are precious in His eyes.

Nothing else matters
It's all in what He wrote
We are His workmanship
In Him lies our hope.

He breathed into us
Told us where to put all our trust
Acknowledging Him
He takes the lead
And reminds us that
You Are Enough
You Are Enough
You Are Enough
You
Are
Enough
We are enough.

# *I AM JUST ME*

They're just jealous.
That's what my parents would tell me whenever others
bullied or made fun of me.
Jealous? I'd ask.
Jealous of what?
It's JUST me.
I'm JUST me.

Just.
Just me.
Who knew that being JUST me would make others so
fearful of me.
Not by what I did, not by what I said
But by just being me.

You see, the thing about me is that, that's all I am.
Me.
No one else
Nothing else
Just
Me.

Who knew that being me, would lead to others trying to
imitate me?
Competing with me?
Doing their best to take parts…of…me?

You can't be me, just like I can't be you.
The only difference here is that I would never want to be you.
I'm not perfect by any means, but me being me is something you'll never be.
You'll never win, never succeed,
The game that you're trying to play is played out.
Go about your day.
Go about your way.
I'll be the only one playing ME today.
Today, Tomorrow and forever more.
There will never be a time that you can even the score.
So, bye now, be gone.
I don't wanna, see ya later.
This "Just Me" is no longer assimilating.

*For so long, I tried to meet the image of what others wanted me to be.*
*From "friends" to potential suitors, to coworkers—*
*I hoped that "being" this person, whoever that was, would make others like me, want me, choose…me.*
*I finally got to a point in my healing to be proud of who I was, love myself, and ultimately choose myself.*
*I chose me!*

# *I AM CHOSEN*

I
Choose
Me.

You
See I waited to be seen.
I waited to be chosen.
I waited to be heard
I waited to be noticed
I waited to be valued
I waited to be understood.
I waited to be favored, appreciated, preferred

Waiting
Waiting for a mating
To be chosen for me
To be selected
To be cherished
To be the last nominee.

Not on the bench
Not on the squad
No longer on the team.
Just me
Just myself
Just I

No facade.
Just
M
E
in team.

Do you see me?
Does it really matter?
Greatness stands before you.
But wait…
Perhaps the question isn't just that
Perhaps the real conundrum is
Me seeing me.

Let's unveil the mystery
That is going back in history
That I must insist that me
I
Myself
Understanding the complexities that
Must've taken over me
To truly not realize
That
I
Must be
Proud of who
I
Am

To walk my walk
And
Talk my talk
And
Recognize that
I
Must appreciate the unique qualities
That encompasses me
To create this beautiful
Unity
Of
Self.

This self that goes beyond the lovely outward appearance
Self that creates a safe space of hearing and acceptance
Self that radiates light in a room
Self that builds unbroken bonds that bloom

This self that is wonderfully created to be
Me
In His image has already been seen

Chosen
Selected
Set apart Sanctified for
His purpose
Loved by Him from the start.

I choose me
I choose myself
I choose, I,
I exist
To be seen
To be heard
To be chosen
I
Choose
Me.

*I went through early menopause and with that my
metabolism declined.
My infertility brought weight gain that I hadn't
seen before. It affected my self-esteem, confidence
and many jean sizes.*

*Mentally, I wasn't prepared for it all at once.
I wanted to look in the
mirror and see someone beautiful looking back at
me.*

*Through therapeutic writing, I saw myself again. I
began to finally embrace the "extraness" that my
body was now giving me.
I had to not only embrace it, but also love, value
and appreciate it.*

# *I AM THESE CURVES*

Chocolate
Radiant
Bumps
Humps
Lumps
Rolls

Fat
Curves
Plumpness
Thickness beyond control

It sits up high
Sometimes it sits low
Either way I'm learning to love how it shows.

It may feel like excess
It may look round
It may seem like it's taking over your old body
But don't frown.

The journey to it getting here
Is not to be ignored
You worked for all of this You
earned it for sure.

Take on all of life's gifts
This is one you might miss
If you don't see the beauty of
This
New
Metamorphosis

It's a beauty unlike others
This grown woman thing
Take a chance and embrace it
All the uniqueness it brings

Like the chocolate soft skin
That flows down the body
Like a sweet, sweet river.

Or the curves that it rolls over
creating a beautifully made spongy ripple

Two bumps at the front
One rump in the back
Both make this playground
Ready for play
That's a fact.

This chocolate river that flows
Down this body of curves

Keeps going like a fountain

It pours
Embrace the fat
Embrace the blubber
Embrace the soft silky smoothness
Embrace the chocolate goodness unending.

Loving this transformation
This change of appearance
Trying on the new size
New vibes
New outward presence
Loving this chocolate river
Loving it all
Loving all of me
Including
The new addition of me
That add to my beauty
**That**
**are**
**these**
**curves.**

*I am shy, soft spoken, and an introvert.*
*I was picked on because of my dark skin,*
*my super thick, kinky hair,*
*and my "proper" speaking.*

*At times, I compared myself to others, often*
*wishing I could have straighter hair, a lighter*
*complexion, be more loud, vocal, extroverted*
*— just less like me.*

*One thing that I've finally grown to*
*love is myself.*

*I've learned to love the uniqueness and*
*quirkiness, my flaws, all of me.*

*I'm proud of the woman I've become*
*and*
*I'm thankful for my journey.*

# *I AM WOMAN!*

I
Am
Woman!

From my massive fro
To the gap in my teeth
To the smirk of my smile
To the dimples in my cheeks

I
Am
Woman!

From the curves of my body
To my smooth chocolate skin
From the stride in my step
And the beauty from within

I
Am
Woman!

From skinny minny
To thick thighs
And way more fine

I
Am
Woman!

From looked over
And picked on
To being seen
And called upon

I
Am
Woman!

From innocent
And low self-esteem
To confidence
Now just watch me

I
Am
Woman

From too dark
To hot cocoa pleasure
From too thick of hair
To naturalista

I
Am
Woman

From too quiet
And not loud enough
To speaking up for others
And all whose voices are handcuffed

I
Am
Woman

From the mothers
To the childless
From the wives
To those in their singleness

I
Am
Woman

I am she
She is me
I am her
I am we

**I
Am
Woman!**

# *I AM MY SHINE*

This shine is mine
The sparkle
The glow
All the ways that I flow

Oh, it's mine.

It's bright and blazing
The glimmer that comes from my rays keeps raising

This little light of mine
Oh, I'm definitely gonna let it shine
This shine is fire
And as it continues to get higher
Wave the smoke
Fan the flame
Feel the heat
Watch this
One can't extinguish
That which continues to burn
Continues to flicker
The warmth of my words only intensifies my light, never
dimmers
It builds the vitality

Of my inner tranquility
It ignites this passion inside of me
That I would be
Seen, no longer hiding me
For this shine is divine
Pause
Wait for it
**I have arrived.**

# *<u>I AM CALLED FOR SUCH A TIME AS THIS</u>*

Selected
Chosen
Royalty
For such a time as this

Why
Am
I
Dealing with the pain?
The pain of making a choice
A choice that had to be made.

Why
Am
I
Selected to speak out?
Speak up.
That's not my nature.
I am meek and mild.
Calm and quiet.
No desire to be dramatic.
The spotlight isn't for me.
I'm just minding my business.
But

He says
That your business is my business
So
Here
I
Am.

Here to make a difference
To be a voice for the voiceless
Here to make a difference
As I articulate brilliance.
Brilliance not from me
But from He who sent me.
Walking His walk
Following His moves
Has moved me to the place
That helps others move too.
It may not be physically
It may not be mentally
But perhaps it's moves that move you to want to make
moves too.

You see
We are hand selected
Chosen by Him
Not many
Not all
But those hand-picked.
He does so for a purpose

For a reason only He knows.


So, when He selects you,
And it's your time to shine,
Don't take it lightly
Don't ask why
Don't shirk just work
Don't take it personally
Just be honored and smile
For He has chosen you
To go through
To endure
To stand up
For such a time as this.

# *<u>OH, I AM PROUD TO BE A WOMAN!</u>*

Woman!
The plight
The flight
The stress
The mess

Woman!
She never stops
Can't sit down
Constantly going
Wondering how?

How does she do it?
Get it all together?
Carry her load, your load, their loads and others?

Woman!

Continuing to push through
Juggling all life's complexities and inequities
Brushing off pain, hurt, doubt and despair
Clothing herself with kindness, righteousness, compassion
and care.

Woman!

She must put on THAT face

That can only REPLACE
That which she CAN'T show
Only so she CAN be seen
And not be ERASED.

Woman!

This grown woman thing
It's really a thing
A thing that can't be understood
Unless you were she

She who takes control
Sits back when necessary
Takes action
Makes decisions
Offers a place to retreat.

Retreat
To solitude
A peaceful place
One where she replenishes and rejuvenates

A place where she can piece together her peace

Woman!

She illuminates

As she elevates
To new heights
Ignoring
The
Bait
Of
Hate.

Woman!

The power that **YOU** possess
Is something that **CAN'T** be finessed
It comes with the territory
It comes with the crown
The **throne** is **yours**
**Your time is now**!

Woman!

Continue to radiate
Head up high
Sparkle and shine
Queens you are divine
Because there is nothing
Nothing
Nothing
Like
A
Woman!

# *ABOUT THE AUTHOR:*

*Melissa Felix is an accomplished educator and writer with over a decade of experience teaching elementary students. An Arlington, Texas native, she earned her Bachelor's degree in Sociology from the University of Texas at Arlington and a Master's degree in Educational Leadership from the University of North Texas.*

*While navigating the challenges of Premature Ovarian Failure (POF), Melissa turned to writing as a source of healing and empowerment.*

*Through candid interviews, heartfelt storytelling, and community events, she has created safe spaces for women to share their experiences with infertility and find connection.*

*Her debut book, Silence Speaks, reflects her journey— transforming pain into purpose and silence into strength.*

*Beyond the page, Melissa is a dynamic spoken word artist whose poetry shows have sold out across Texas. She is a proud member of Sigma Gamma Rho Sorority, Inc., an avid supporter of the arts, and believes there is no greater calling than to serve the community in which she calls home in the Dallas Fort-Worth Metroplex area.*

*When she's not writing, traveling, or performing, Melissa enjoys life's simple joys—exploring nature, basking in the rays of the sun, visiting museums, listening to the rhythm of the ocean waves, soaking up live music, and spending time with her Mini Goldendoodle, Simba.*

www.ingramcontent.com/pod-product-compliance
Lightning Source LLC
Chambersburg PA
CBHW060524130626
46553CB00002B/647